William Schaus

American lepidoptera:

Illustrations of new and rare species

William Schaus

American lepidoptera:
Illustrations of new and rare species

ISBN/EAN: 9783337815066

Printed in Europe, USA, Canada, Australia, Japan

Cover: Foto ©ninafisch / pixelio.de

More available books at **www.hansebooks.com**

PART 1. | NOVEMBER 1892.

AMERICAN LEPIDOPTERA:

ILLUSTRATIONS

OF

NEW AND RARE SPECIES.

BY

W. SCHAUS, Jun., F.Z.S.

CONTENTS.

LONDON:

R. H. PORTER, 18 PRINCES STREET, CAVENDISH SQUARE, W.

1892.

AMERICAN LEPIDOPTERA.

―――――▸◂•▸◂―――― -- ―

Fam. ZYGÆNIDÆ.

Subfam. *PYROMORPHINÆ.*

Harrisina janeira. (Tab. I. fig. 1.)

Harrisina janeira, Schaus, Proc. Zool. Soc. Lond. 1892, p. 272.

Dull greenish black; the second and third abdominal segments bright red.
Expanse 26 millim.

Hab. Petropolis, Brazil.

Harrisina eminens. (Tab. I. fig. 2.)

Harrisina eminens, Schaus, Proc. Zool. Soc. Lond. 1892, p. 272.

Bluish black; the base of the wings yellow, and on the primaries a yellow mark crossing the wing from the subcostal vein at about two thirds from the base and extending to the outer margin just above the inner angle; this mark is somewhat in the shape of a **T**, having the upper portion along the subcostal vein. At the base of the abdomen a short lateral yellow streak.

Expanse 28 millim.

Hab. Tijuca, Brazil.

This species bears a very strong resemblance to *Dycladia correbioides*, Felder.

Subfam. *EUCHROMIINÆ.*

Eupyra psittacus. (Tab. I. fig. 6.)

Eupyra psittacus, Schaus, Proc. Zool. Soc. Lond. 1892, p. 273.

Primaries above dull metallic green, with the outer margin broadly black; under-
November 1892.   B

neath bright metallic green, except the apical third, which is black. Secondaries above black, the costal margin bright metallic green and the inner margin shot with bluish green; underneath bright metallic green, with a very narrow black outer margin. Head and thorax black; a white spot behind the eyes, and six white spots on the thorax. Abdomen above black, with a subdorsal row of white spots, the one on the first segment being much larger than the others; laterally metallic green; underneath brownish black, with two rows of large white spots. Coxæ white. Antennæ black.

Expanse 41 millim. Four males.

Hab. Peru.

Eupyra consors. (Tab. I. fig. 7.)

Eupyra consors, Schaus, Proc. Zool. Soc. Lond. 1892, p. 273.

Primaries above dark green with a golden tinge, the outer margin broadly black; near the end of the cell a small hyaline spot; underneath the same as above, but of a brighter metallic green, and there is a second small spot denuded of scales just beyond the cell, and in some specimens a third similar spot below the middle of the median vein. Secondaries above black, the costal margin bright green, at the base of the inner margin a small white spot and a small semihyaline streak in the cell; underneath bright green, with the spots as above and a narrow black outer margin. Thorax black, with white spots as in *E. psittacus*. Abdomen above black, golden between the segments, and a subdorsal row of small white spots; laterally golden; underneath brown, with an outer row of white spots.

Expanse 44 millim.

Hab. Peru.

Eupyra aurata. (Tab. I. fig. 8.)

Eupyra aurata, Schaus, Proc. Zool. Soc. Lond. 1892, p. 273.

Wings above dull golden green. The inner margin of the secondaries black. Underneath the same as above, with the apex and the outer margin of the primaries dark brown. Head black, two small white spots on the frons and a similar spot behind each antenna. Thorax black with white spots. Body golden, with a black subdorsal band and a narrow black transverse line separating each segment; laterally a broad brown band with a row of large silver spots; dorsally there are two small white spots on the first segment.

Expanse 42 millim. Two females.

Hab. Peru.

Eupyra bacchans. (Tab. I. fig. 5.)

Eupyra bacchans, Schaus, Proc. Zool. Soc. Lond. 1892, p. 274.

Primaries above dark green, with a broad black outer margin and a white spot at the base of the costa; underneath the wings are more of a dull golden green, the outer margins blackish brown. Secondaries above black, a few dark green scales between the second and third median nervules; underneath golden green. Antennæ black with white tips. Thorax black, two white spots mingled with bluish scales on the collar and similar spots on the thorax. Abdomen black, a subdorsal and two lateral rows of small white spots, each spot having anteriorly a cluster of bright blue scales.

Expanse, ♂ 45 millim., ♀ 48 millim.

Hab. Peru.

Isanthrene gaza. (Tab. I. fig. 9.)

Isanthrene gaza, Schaus, Proc. Zool. Soc. Lond. 1892, p. 274.

Primaries yellowish hyaline, darker along the costal and inner margins; the outer and inner margins with a very narrow black border, the apices broadly black; at the base of the wings a few blue scales. Secondaries above yellowish hyaline, the outer margin very narrowly bordered with black, the inner margin very narrowly orange; underneath the same as above, with the costal margins of a much deeper yellow. Frons orange. Metallic blue spots at the base of the antennæ. Collar orange, with two black spots having bright blue centres. Tegulæ orange inwardly, black outwardly. Thorax black, with two patches of metallic blue scales. Abdomen above with the first segment yellow, the following segments orange with two rows of transversely elongated metallic blue spots bordered with black, the black meeting subdorsally: these spots are placed on the posterior portion of each segment; laterally are similar blue and black markings; underneath, abdomen pale yellow.

Expanse 37 millim. ♀.

Hab. Peru.

Gymnelia serra. (Tab. I. fig. 10.)

Gymnelia serra, Schaus, Proc. Zool. Soc. Lond. 1892, p. 274.

Primaries yellowish hyaline, the margins broadly bordered with black. A black mark at the end of the cell. Secondaries whitish hyaline, the outer margin broadly black. Antennæ, head, and thorax black; two small dark metallic blue spots on the collar. Abdomen velvety black, with a lateral row of dull red spots separated by clusters of dark metallic blue scales.

Expanse 40 millim. ♀.

Hab. Rio Janeiro, Brazil.

Gartha dalsa, sp. nov. (Tab. I. fig. 15.)

Primaries hyaline with the margins narrowly black, and a broad black space at the base spotted with metallic-blue scales · at the end of the cell a narrow black transverse streak. Secondaries hyaline with the outer margin black, broadly so at the anal angle. Antennæ black. Head black; frons white with a few blue scales, and there are a few white scales behind the antennæ. Collar black, with two large white spots broadly shaded with metallic-blue scales. Thorax black, dorsally shaded with dark blue. Abdomen dorsally black, with a subdorsal row of small blue spots; on the first segment are four large white spots, and on the second segment three, all these spots being anteriorly bordered with blue scales. Body underneath black shaded with dark blue; at the base of the abdomen a broad white transverse band. Coxæ white.

Expanse 34 millim.

Hab. One specimen received from the province of Sta. Catharina, Brazil.

There is also a specimen of this species in the collection of H. Druce, Esq., taken by Buckley in Ecuador.

Pseudomya tijuca. (Tab. I. fig. 3.)

Pseudomya tijuca, Schaus, Proc. Zool. Soc. Lond. 1892, p. 275.

Female. Primaries semihyaline black. Secondaries hyaline, darker towards the outer margin. Head black; thorax orange; abdomen black above, whitish underneath.

Expanse 30 millim.

Hab. Tijuca, Brazil.

Pseudomya pellucida. (Tab. I. fig. 4.)

Pseudomya pellucida, Schaus, Proc. Zool. Soc. Lond. 1892, p. 274.

Male. Primaries with the basal half semihyaline, black, the apical half hyaline. Secondaries hyaline, a few dark scales along the costal margin. Body black, subdorsally velvety black.

Expanse 20–24 millim.

Female. Primaries entirely semihyaline black. Secondaries slightly more transparent. Body as in the male.

Expanse 20 millim.

Hab. Rio Janeiro, Brazil.

A very common species in December and January.

Cosmosoma harpalyce. (Tab. I. fig. 11.)

Cosmosoma harpalyce, Schaus, Proc. Zool. Soc. Lond. 1892, p. 273.

Primaries hyaline, the inner and outer margins very narrowly black, the apex broadly black, a black spot at the end of the cell. Secondaries hyaline, the outer margin narrowly black, more widely so at the apex and along the inner margin. Antennæ, head, and thorax black, the latter reddish outwardly. Abdomen above dull black, with two reddish spots at the base ; underneath yellowish, except the last two segments, which are black.

Expanse 34 millim.

Hab. Petropolis, Brazil.

Dycladia catherina. (Tab. I. fig. 12.)

Dycladia catherina, Schaus, Proc. Zool. Soc. Lond. 1892, p. 275.

Wings hyaline, the apices black, the margins very narrowly black. Antennæ, head, thorax, and abdomen black. A large crimson spot on each side of the thorax, and a round crimson spot on each side of the fourth segment of the abdomen.

Expanse 26 millim.   ♂ .

Hab. Santa Cathariua, Brazil.

Dycladia rogenhoferi. (Tab. I. fig. 13.)

Dycladia rogeuhoferi, Schaus, Proc. Zool. Soc. Lond. 1892, p. 275.

Wings hyaline. Primaries with the apices and fringe black; a little yellow at the base of the wing. Frons white. Head, thorax, and abdomen bright yellow, with a subdorsal black line.

Expanse 19 millim.

Hab. Petropolis, Brazil.

This species is most closely allied to *Dycladia felderi*, Druce, but differs in the subdorsal markings and the smaller extent of black at the apices of the primaries.

Dycladia epimetheus. (Tab. I. fig. 14.)

Dycladia epimetheus, Schaus, Proc. Zool. Soc. Lond. 1892, p. 275.

Wings hyaline, with the margins rather broadly black, especially the apices; base of the primaries red; a small black mark at the end of the cell of the same wing. Head black. Thorax and base of the abdomen, laterally, red; abdomen otherwise black.

Expanse 25 millim.   ♀ .

Hab. Nova Friburgo, Brazil.

Subfam. *TRICHURINÆ.*

Syntrichura doeri. (Tab. I. fig. 16.)

Syntrichura doeri, Schaus, Proc. Zool. Soc. Lond. 1892, p. 276.

Wings hyaline. Primaries narrowly margined with black. Secondaries having only the costa and apex black. Head and thorax black, with a yellow lateral streak. Abdomen black, with a lateral row of yellow spots. Abdomen below whitish.

Expanse 21 millim. ♂.

Hab. Petropolis, Brazil.

Fam. ARCTIIDÆ.

Subfam. *CHARIDEINÆ.*

Aclytia petra. (Tab. I. fig. 17.)

Aclytia petra, Schaus, Proc. Zool. Soc. Lond. 1892, p. 276.

Primaries brownish black, with all the veins clearly defined. Secondaries hyaline, with a broad black margin. Head and thorax black ; a metallic blue spot between the antennæ. Abdomen dorsally black, laterally metallic blue, underneath white. Legs black ; joints and coxæ white.

Expanse 32 millim.

Hab. Peru.

Aclytia hecale. (Tab. I. fig. 18.)

Aclytia hecale, Schaus, Proc. Zool. Soc. Lond. 1892, p. 277.

Primaries dull black, faintly hyaline in the disk and darkest on the margins and at the end of the cell. Secondaries hyaline, with a broad black margin. Antennæ, head, and thorax black ; two crimson spots behind the antennæ. Abdomen black, with a lateral band of metallic blue. Base of all the legs bright crimson.

Expanse 39 millim. ♀.

Hab. Petropolis, Brazil.

Cyanopepla inachia. (Tab. I. fig. 19.)

Charidea inachia, Schaus, Proc. Zool. Soc. Lond. 1892, p. 277.

Female. Primaries above velvety black, with a large orange space extending in its anterior portion from the base along the subcostal vein to beyond the cell, and posteriorly along the submedian vein to close upon the inner angle, and divided by two black lines, one just below the median vein, the other just above the submedian ; a small black transverse mark at the end of the cell. Secondaries velvety black.

Underneath black, with a large triangular orange spot on the primaries. Head and thorax black. Abdomen above steel-blue, with two black dorsal lines; underneath black.

Expanse 33 millim.

Hab. Petropolis, Brazil.

Metriophyla lena. (Tab. I. fig. 24.)
Metriophyla lena, Schaus, Proc. Zool. Soc. Lond. 1892, p. 277.

Primaries above velvety black, fringe white; the basal third of the costal margin narrowly white. Secondaries above black, glossed with dark blue; the outer margin narrowly, the apex broadly, white. Underneath: wings black, glossed with dark blue; the apices and outer margins white. Antennæ black. Head crimson. Frons white. Thorax black, with a white spot on either side. Abdomen black above, tinged with dark blue; underneath black, with a white ventral line. Anus crimson. Legs black exteriorly, white inwardly.

Expanse 36 millim.

Hab. Peru.

Heliura venata. (Tab. I. fig. 20.)
♀. *Episcepsis venata*, Butler, Ill. Lep. Het. B. M. i. p. 49, t. 16. f. 7.
♂. *Heliura ælia*, Schaus, Ent. Amer. v. p. 90.

Male. Primaries dull brown and apparently slightly transparent, so that all the veins and nervules are distinctly marked in a darker shade of brown. Base of wings, a spot at the end of the cell, the apices, the outer margins, and a blotch at the internal angle also of a darker shade. Secondaries whitish towards the base, otherwise brown-black; a tuft of white hairs in anal fold. Wings underneath dull black, with all the veins and nervules distinctly showing. Antennæ black. Head brown, with two bright red spots behind the antennæ. Thorax brown, underneath a crimson spot. Abdomen dorsally metallic blue, with narrow black transverse bands between the segments, and a tuft of long brown hairs dorsally on first three segments. On abdomen underneath a large white spot.

Expanse 30 millim. One male.

Hab. Paso de San Juan, Mexico.

Euplesia elissa. (Tab. I. fig. 21.)
Automolis elissa, Schaus, Proc. Zool. Soc. Lond. 1892, p. 277.

Wings pale yellow, secondaries slightly hyaline. Head orange. Collar and thorax yellow. Abdomen dorsally black, except fourth and fifth segments, which are orange with two black subdorsal spots; abdomen laterally and underneath orange, with three lateral black spots on the third, fourth, and fifth segments.

Expanse 54 millim ♀

Hab. Rio Janeiro, Brazil.

Galethalea peruviana. (Tab. I. fig. 22.)

Galethalea peruviana, Schaus, Proc. Zool. Soc. Lond. 1892, p. 277.

Male. Primaries above white, shaded with greenish grey ; along the costal margin five large irregular black spots, also three similar spots on the inner margin and three small black spots on the outer margin ; underneath the spots are suffused and occupy nearly the entire wing, forming a broad submarginal band. Secondaries above white, slightly hyaline, the apex broadly, the outer margin faintly, clouded with black ; underneath the same, with a long black spot on the costal margin. Antennæ black, with a broad white space near the base and also near the tip. Head white. Thorax white, spotted with black. Abdomen above brown, the last three segments yellow with subdorsal black spots ; underneath white. Anus black.

Expanse 32 millim.

Hab. Peru.

Subfam. *CTENUCHINÆ.*

Leucopsumis braganza. (Tab. II. fig. 26.)

Melanchroia braganza, Schaus, Proc. Zool. Soc. Lond. 1892, p. 288.

Primaries velvety black, the veins clearly defined, especially towards the base; a transverse subapical white band. Secondaries black, glossed with dark blue; fringe white. Underneath black, glossed with dark blue ; veins on secondaries whitish ; transverse white band on the primaries as on the upper surface. Head black above, orange underneath. Thorax blue-black, with a few faint whitish streaks. Abdomen blue-black ; white underneath in the male.

Expanse 38 millim.

Hab. Rio Janeiro, Brazil.

Very closely allied to *L. circe*, Cramer.

Leucopsumis palmeira. (Tab. II. fig. 24.)

Melanchroia palmeira, Schaus, Proc. Zool. Soc. Lond. 1892, p. 288.

Primaries black; a white subapical elongated spot. Secondaries bluish black ; the apex white. Underneath the same. Body black ; the abdomen slightly glossed with blue.

Expanse 35 millim. ♀.

Hab. Palmeiras, Rio Janeiro.

Subfam. *PHÆGOPTERINÆ.*

Amaxia hebe. (Tab. I. fig. 28.)

Amaxia hebe, Schaus, Proc. Zool. Soc. Lond. 1892, p. 278.

Male. Primaries above pale yellow, a large purplish-brown spot broadly bordered with roseate occupying the base of the wings for one third from the base along the subcostal vein, and the entire inner margin, except a small yellow spot about the middle of the inner margin. At the apices two small brownish spots surrounded by roseate. The intermediate yellow space with widely separated and very small indistinct pinkish spots. Secondaries above slightly hyaline, rose colour, whitish along the costal margin. Underneath whitish, the base of the primaries roseate, the apical spots smaller than on the upperside. Head yellow above, crimson underneath. Collar yellow; thorax and abdomen dorsally crimson, underneath whitish.

Expanse 33 millim.

Hab. Rio Janeiro, Brazil.

Amaxia pyga. (Tab. I. fig. 27.)

Amaxia pyga, Schaus, Proc. Zool. Soc. Lond. 1892, p. 279.

Female. Primaries above pale yellow; the entire basal portion to the inner angle, except the costa, purplish brown, faintly mottled with red, especially on the veins and the margins of this dark space; four elongated brown spots, exteriorly shaded with red, at the apex; a marginal row of small brown spots, and a few other similar minute spots scattered over the yellow portion : underneath pale yellow, with the entire inner margin and base, except the costa, dull brown ; four brown spots at the apex. Secondaries above brown, the costal margin and apex yellow; underneath yellow. Head and collar yellow. Thorax and abdomen dorsally brown. Abdomen underneath white. Legs yellow.

Expanse 33 millim.

Hab. Rio Janeiro, Brazil.

Scaptius juno. (Tab. II. fig. 3.)

Scaptius juno, Schaus, Proc. Zool. Soc. Lond. 1892, p. 279.

Female. Primaries pale purplish brown, a white spot at the base near the inner margin, beyond this a transverse yellow band from the subcostal to the submedian vein, and on this band is a wavy reddish line ; close beyond it and just above the inner margin are three small yellowish spots ; a submarginal row of four hyaline spots and a marginal row of small irregular yellow spots. Fringe alternately yellow and brown.

November 1892.   c

Secondaries roseate, fringe yellow. Head yellow. Thorax brownish. Abdomen fawn-colour.

Expanse 39 millim

Hab. Petropolis, Brazil.

Idalus ortus. (Tab. II. fig. 1.)

Idalus ortus, Schaus, Proc. Zool. Soc. Lond. 1892, p. 279.

Female. White, the disk of the primaries slightly iridescent, a few black specks at the base of the primaries, and some short black marks just beyond the cell, a conspicuous black dot near the outer margin below the apex. Head and thorax white, pinkish between the antennæ. Abdomen white, dorsally shaded with pink.

Expanse 37 millim.

Hab. Rio Janeiro, Brazil.

Eucereon clementsi, sp. nov. (Tab. I. fig. 25.)

Primaries above black, at the base three small pinkish spots, an extrabasal transverse angular pink line, some irregular pinkish marks in the cell, an outer irregular transverse pink band, divided in its anterior portion by a black streak, a submarginal row of angular pink streaks, and a marginal pink line broken by the veins. Secondaries above smoky black, with the disk whitish hyaline. Underneath the primaries are dull black with a few pinkish shades below the costa, and the outer line is represented by a few pinkish spots. Antennæ black ; head black ; a crimson line behind the head. Thorax black, with a red spot posteriorly. Abdomen above crimson, except the first segments subdorsally and the anus, which are black ; abdomen laterally black, ventrally crimson. Legs black, spotted with red.

Expanse 35 millim.

Hab. St. Lucia, W.I.

I have named this species after Mr. W. G. Clements, of Rochester, to whom I am indebted for a very fine specimen.

Eucereon ladas. (Tab. I. fig. 26.)

Eucereon ladas, Schaus, Proc. Zool. Soc. Lond. 1892, p. 278.

Male. Primaries grey ; the veins, a median and a marginal angulated band, some streaks between the veins on the extreme margin, and a few shades at the base of the wings dark brown ; there is a minute spot in the middle of the cell connected with a similar spot at the end of the cell by a fine black line. Secondaries dark brown. Head and thorax grey, with brown spots on the collar. Abdomen brown dorsally, the last three segments yellow ; underneath two white streaks.

The *female* is paler on the primaries, and the secondaries are greyish with darker margins.

Expanse 28 millim.

Hab. Rio Janeiro, Brazil.

Theages vestalis. (Tab. I. fig. 23.)
Theages vestalis, Schaus, Proc. Zool. Soc. Lond. 1892, p. 278.

White; wings semihyaline, slightly iridescent.

Expanse 22 millim.

Hab. Peru.

Ameles byblis. (Tab. II. fig. 2.)
Ameles byblis, Schaus, Proc. Zool. Soc. Lond. 1892, p. 279.

Primaries above dark brown, a space at the base, and a large subapical space on the outer margin, testaceous, with two rows of paler spots. About the middle of the costal margin are two nearly contiguous testaceous spots, and likewise two about the middle of the inner margin. Secondaries above blackish, a yellow basal spot on the costa. Underneath dull brown, orange at the base of the four wings, and orange shades along the basal half of the costal and inner margins of the primaries. The subapical patch on the outer margin as on the upperside. Head and thorax yellow, with two broad brown bands. Abdomen dorsally dark brown, laterally yellow, with two rows of black spots; underneath whitish.

Expanse 37 millim.

Hab. Corcovado, Rio Janeiro.

Sychesia hartmanni. (Tab. III. fig. 10.)
Sychesia hartmanni, Schaus, Proc. Zool. Soc. Lond. 1892, p. 280.

Primaries dark brown, an indistinct wavy submarginal shade. Secondaries black-brown, faintly hyaline in the disk. Head and thorax above brown, an orange spot at the base of the antennæ; thorax underneath orange. Abdomen dorsally black, laterally orange, underneath brown.

Expanse 40 millim.

Hab. Petropolis, Brazil.

Sychesia janeira. (Tab. III. fig. 14.)
Sychesia janeira, Schaus, Proc. Zool. Soc. Lond. 1892, p. 280.

Male. Primaries above light brown, with numerous transverse pale streaks, all the veins orange-brown; secondaries yellowish white, black on the margins. Head and thorax brown, the collar edged with dull orange. Abdomen dorsally orange, the first

c 2

segment unspotted, the following three with large transverse black spots, the other segments with subdorsal black spots; abdomen underneath brown, wavy along the sides where confluent with the orange. The anus dark brown.

The *female* differs in having the secondaries entirely dull brownish black.

Expanse 52 millim.

Hab. Rio Janeiro, Brazil.

Phægoptera notata. (Tab. III. fig. 6.)

Phægoptera notata, Schaus, Proc. Zool. Soc. Lond. 1892, p. 281.

Primaries brown, with three large yellowish-white spots on the costal margin. Secondaries whitish, with the veins and margins brown, and a yellow spot at the base on the costal margin. Head and thorax brown; two yellow dots on the collar, and a large yellow spot on either side of the thorax. Abdomen black dorsally, with narrow crimson transverse bands; underneath brown, with two rows of white spots.

Expanse 51 millim.

Hab. Petropolis, Brazil.

Phægoptera ursina. (Tab. III. fig. 15.)

Phægoptera ursina, Schaus, Proc. Zool. Soc. Lond. 1892, p. 281.

Primaries rich brown; a large irregular whitish spot at the base of the wings; a whitish spot on the costa at a third from the base, and a large whitish spot extending from the costa just beyond the middle of the wing, and inwardly contiguous to a small pinkish crescent at the end of the cell; an irregular and sometimes broken band of white along the outer margin, extending from just below the apex to the inner angle. Secondaries above duller brown, the costa mottled with white. Underneath pale brown, the spots on the primaries less distinct, and on the secondaries there are two large whitish spots on the costal margin. Head and thorax pale brown, with a broad whitish band on either side. Abdomen above pink, with a subdorsal row of black spots; underneath white; laterally a row of black spots.

Expanse, ♂ 42 millim., ♀ 58 millim.

Hab. Rio Janeiro, Brazil.

Phægoptera granifera. (Tab. III. fig. 4.)

Phægoptera granifera, Schaus, Proc. Zool. Soc. Lond. 1892, p. 281.

Primaries dark brown, crossed by six rows of yellowish-brown spots; a small white space at the base, another on the middle of the costal margin, and a third subapical. Secondaries uniform blackish brown. Head and thorax brown, spotted with yellow and white. Abdomen dorsally brown on the first four segments, subsequently orange; underneath whitish, laterally orange with some minute whitish spots.

Expanse 45 millim.

Hab. Petropolis, Brazil.

Ecpantheria pellucida. (Tab. III. figg. 11, ♂; 12, ♀.)

Ecpantheria pellucida, Schaus, Proc. Zool. Soc. Lond. 1892, p. 282.

Male. Primaries hyaline, except the base and the costal and inner margins, which are white spotted with grey edged with black. Secondaries hyaline, except along the costal and inner margins, which are white, the costal margin being spotted with black. In some specimens there is a black spot at the anal angle. Head and thorax light grey, with darker spots edged with black. Abdomen dorsally bluish black; ventrally white.

Expanse 55 millim.

The *female* has the body as in the male. The primaries are white crossed by six rows of large grey spots edged with black. The secondaries are black, with the costal and outer margins white spotted with grey, and there is a white band starting from the costal margin beyond the middle and extending halfway across the wing.

Expanse 62 millim.

Hab. Rio Janeiro, Brazil.

Fam. LITHOSIIDÆ.

Trichomelia celenna. (Tab. II. fig. 5.)

Trichomelia celenna, Schaus, Proc. Zool. Soc. Lond. 1892, p. 284.

Primaries above white, all the veins grey; the costal margin very broadly grey for two thirds from the base; a large grey space on the inner margin near the angle. Secondaries above grey. Underneath all the wings grey. Head and thorax whitish. Abdomen dark grey.

Expanse 23 millim.

Hab. Rio Janeiro, Brazil.

Cisthene petrovna. (Tab. II. fig. 4.)

Cisthene petrovna, Schaus, Proc. Zool. Soc. Lond. 1892, p. 284.

Primaries above grey, slightly paler at the base, with the veins darker; a broad white median band, and a white spot at the apex. Secondaries grey; towards the base and along the inner margin yellowish. Underneath: primaries grey; secondaries whitish, with the apex broadly grey. Head grey, collar yellow. Thorax grey. Abdomen yellow.

Expanse 01 millim.

Hab. Petropolis, Brazil.

Brycea peruviana. (Tab. II. fig. 16.)

Brycea peruviana, Schaus, Proc. Zool. Soc. Lond. 1892, p. 283.

Wings black; a broad orange longitudinal streak from the base to nearly the outer margin on both the primaries and secondaries, the former having also a transverse subapical orange spot. Head and thorax black. Tegulæ orange. Abdomen black, orange laterally.

Expanse 35 millim.

Hab. Peru.

Ardonea metallica. (Tab. II. fig. 8.)

Ardonea metallica, Schaus, Proc. Zool. Soc. Lond. 1892, p. 284.

Primaries above greenish black. Secondaries metallic blue. Underneath all the wings metallic bluish green. Head and thorax black. Abdomen dark green.

Expanse 30 millim.

Hab. Peru.

Eudule venata. (Tab. II. fig. 7.)

Eudule venata, Schaus, Proc. Zool. Soc. Lond. 1892, p. 284.

Wings orange-red; the primaries with the apex and outer margin black; the subcostal and median veins black; a black streak in the cell, and a long black streak below the median vein; a transverse subapical black line from the costa to the middle of the outer margin. Secondaries with the apex broadly black; the outer margin narrowly black. Body orange.

Expanse 20 millim.

Hab. Peru.

Eudule aurata. (Tab. II. fig. 6.)

Eudule aurata, Schaus, Proc. Zool. Soc. Lond. 1892, p. 284.

Primaries above golden yellow; the subcostal vein and base of median vein black; a large dusky circle on the outer half of the wing connected by a dusky line with the inner angle. Secondaries above golden yellow; an irregular dusky line starting from the base and following the contour of the wing to the anal angle. Underneath the wings are yellow, the costal margin of the primaries black. Body yellow.

Expanse 25 millim.

Hab. Rio Janeiro, Brazil.

Very similar to *Eudule citrosa*, Hübner, which differs in having all the veins along the outer margins black.

Fam. CYLLOPODIDÆ.

Virbia varians. (Tab. II. fig. 19.)
Virbia varians, Schaus, Proc. Zool. Soc. Lond. 1892, p. 284.

Primaries above brown; at the base a broad but short longitudinal streak, and beyond this a white spot. Sometimes the spot is absent and at other times absorbed by the longitudinal streak. Secondaries above orange, with broad black costal and outer margins. Underneath the wings are orange, with the costal and outer margins broadly brown. Head and thorax brown. Body orange, black subdorsally and below.

Expanse 31 millim.

Hab. Peru.

Allied to *Virbia brevilinea*, Walker.

Virbia parva. (Tab. II. fig. 15.)
Virbia parva, Schaus, Proc. Zool. Soc. Lond. 1892, p. 285.

Primaries above brown; underneath orange, with brown margins, the outer being the broadest. Secondaries above black; a broad orange band from the base to nearly the outer margin, just below the apex; the inner margin and anal angle narrowly orange: underneath the same as above. Head and thorax brown. Abdomen black dorsally, orange laterally, white underneath.

Expanse 25 millim.

Hab. Peru.

Allied to *Virbia minuta*, Felder.

Lyces maera. (Tab. II. fig. 17.)
Lyces maera, Schaus, Proc. Zool. Soc. Lond. 1892, p. 285.

Primaries above black; a transverse orange band from the middle of the costal margin to the inner angle: underneath black, the transverse band much broader, and two greyish streaks at the base of the wing. Secondaries above orange; the costal margin narrowly, the outer and inner margins very broadly black: underneath the same, except that the inner margin is also orange, and there is a white streak on the costal margin at its base. Head and thorax black. Abdomen black dorsally; laterally a narrow yellow streak; underneath white.

Expanse 00 millim.

Hab. Petropolis, Brazil.

Gangamela aymara. (Tab. II. fig. 9, ♀.)

Gangamela aymara, Schaus, Proc. Zool. Soc. Lond. 1892, p. 285.

Male. Primaries above bright yellow; the base black; the costal and subcostal veins finely black; the apex and outer margin broadly black; the inner margin narrowly black and glossed with dark blue: underneath similar, except that a portion of the base and inner margin are pearl-white instead of black and there is no blue gloss. Secondaries above black, glossed with blue at the base; yellow towards the apex, which is itself black: underneath pearl-white; the costal margin yellow; the apex narrowly black. Head black; frons white. Thorax dark blue. Abdomen above blue, with a subdorsal yellow line; underneath white.

Expanse 24 millim.

The *female* has the primaries above as in the male. The secondaries above are entirely dull black, glossed with blue at the base and along the inner margin; underneath the pearly white is replaced by black and the yellow margin of the secondaries is very indistinct. The abdomen is also black underneath.

Expanse 29 millim.

Hab. Peru.

Scea solaris. (Tab. II. fig. 14.)

Scea solaris, Schaus, Proc. Zool. Soc. Lond. 1892, p. 285.

Primaries black; a large yellow space extending from the base to close to the centre of the outer margin; this space follows anteriorly along the costa to beyond the cell, and then crosses the wing obliquely; the veins and a conspicuous streak in the cell are also black. Secondaries black; a yellow streak beginning towards the end of the cell and extending beyond it. Underside the same as the upper. Body dull black.

Expanse 33 millim.

Hab. Peru.

Darna inca. (Tab. II. fig. 10.)

Darna inca, Schaus, Proc. Zool. Soc. Lond. 1892, p. 286.

Male. Primaries above velvety black, shaded with metallic blue at the base and along the inner margin; a broad orange band crosses the wing from the middle of the costal margin to nearly the inner angle: underneath as on the upper surface, the inner margin, however, denuded of scales. Secondaries above having the anterior half denuded, greyish, with the male sexual gland; posterior half black; along the inner margin bluish; underneath pale metallic green, the outer margin black. Body metallic blue.

The *female* differs in having the secondaries black, and the metallic colour of the inner margins more extended.

Expanse 35 millim.

Hab. Peru.

Allied to *Darna colorata*, Walk., but differing in the shape of the orange mark on the primaries.

Cyllopoda dubia. (Tab. II. fig. 25.)

Flavinia dubia, Schaus, Proc. Zool. Soc. Lond. 1892, p. 286.

Primaries black, a large yellow space at the base confined within the subcostal and submedian veins; a large subapical elongated yellow spot. Secondaries yellow, with all the margins black. Underside the same. Body black; thorax and abdomen laterally yellow.

Expanse 34 millim.

Hab. Corcovado, Rio Janeiro.

Cyllopoda darna. (Tab. II. fig. 22.)

Flavinia darna, Schaus, Proc. Zool. Soc. Lond. 1892, p. 286.

Very similar to *Flavinia dubia*, Schaus; the subapical spot smaller in proportion, and it is easily recognized from that species by its smaller size and white abdomen underneath.

Expanse 22 millim.

Hab. Nova Friburgo, Brazil.

Cyllopoda janeira. (Tab. II. fig. 20.)

Flavinia janeira, Schaus, Proc. Zool. Soc. Loud. 1892, p. 286.

Primaries above black, a long yellow spot at the base confined within the median and submedian veins; a subapical roundish yellow spot; the extreme apex white. Secondaries yellow with black margins, except the base of the inner and costal margins; underneath the same. Body black; collar yellow. Abdomen with a lateral yellow stripe and underneath white.

Expanse 34 millim.

Hab. Rio Janeiro, Brazil.

Most nearly allied to *Flavinia approximans*, Walker, but differs in the white apices

November 1892. D

of the primaries, and the costal margins of the secondaries, which in *F. approximans* are broadly black, with a short yellow basal streak.

Cyllopoda quicha. (Tab. II. fig. 23.)

Flavinia quicha, Schaus, Proc. Zool. Soc. Lond. 1892, p. 286.

Primaries black; a basal oblong spot confined within the median and submedian veins, and an oblong subapical yellow spot; apices faintly tipped with white. Secondaries yellow; the outer margin broadly black; the costal margin yellow; a subcostal ill-defined black band from the base to the apex. Body black. Abdomen laterally yellow, underneath white.

Expanse 31 millim.

Hab. Peru.

Closely allied to *Flavinia isis*, Hübner, but has broader margins to the secondaries and is a smaller insect.

Cyllopoda chibcha. (Tab. II. fig. 21.)

Flavinia chibcha, Schaus, Proc. Zool. Soc. Lond. 1892, p. 287.

Primaries above black; an oblong yellow spot at the base confined within the median and submedian veins; an elongated subapical yellow spot. Secondaries yellow; the outer margin broadly black, but abruptly narrowing near the anal angle; the costal margin yellow, in most specimens with a black line from the base to the apex; underneath the same, but the black marginal border of the secondaries ceases abruptly before reaching the anal angle. Thorax black; tegulæ orange. Abdomen black dorsally; a yellow stripe laterally; white underneath.

Expanse 25 millim.

Hab. Peru.

Fam. MELAMERIDÆ.

Mennis sceata. (Tab. II. fig. 11.)

Mennis sceata, Schaus, Proc. Zool. Soc. Lond. 1892, p. 287.

Primaries orange; the costa finely, the inner margin narrowly, the apex broadly, and the outer margin black, all the veins finely black. Secondaries black, slightly greyish along the inner margin. Head, thorax, and abdomen black.

Expanse 25 millim.

Hab. Peru.

Mennis cytherea. (Tab. II. fig. 12.)

Mennis cytherea, Schaus, Proc. Zool. Soc. Lond. 1892, p. 287.

Wings above orange-red; all the veins black; the apex and outer margins of the primaries narrowly black; the costal margin of the secondaries broadly black. Fringe black. Body black.

Expanse 23 millim.

Hab. Peru.

Mennis una. (Tab. II. fig. 13.)

Mennis una, Schaus, Proc. Zool. Soc. Lond. 1892, p. 287.

Red; the costal and outer margins narrowly black on the primaries; also a few black specks on the veins near the apex. Secondaries with only the outer margins black.

Expanse 22 millim.

Hab. Petropolis, Brazil.

Nelo caullama. (Tab. II. fig. 18.)

Nelo caullama, Schaus, Proc. Zool. Soc. Lond. 1892, p. 288.

Primaries red; the costal and inner margins narrowly, the apex and outer margin broadly black. Secondaries black. Body black.

Expanse 30 millim.

Hab. Peru.

This species closely resembles *Nelo coccineata*, Walker, but differs in the shape and extent of the red.

Fam. CERATOCAMPIDÆ.

Syssisphinx basirei. (Tab. III. fig. 5.)

Syssphinx basirei, Schaus, Proc. Zool. Soc. Lond. 1892, p. 289.

Primaries above fawn-colour at the base and along the outer margin, the median space darker, and separated from the paler portions by a basal and marginal dark brown line; almost the entire median spaces from the subcostal to the submedian vein vitreous, here and there flecked with opaque clusters of scales. Secondaries fawn-colour, with a dark marginal line, beyond which the wing is slightly darker than at the base; the disk of the wings occupied by large vitreous patches as on the primaries.

D 2

Body fawn-colour, slightly darker on the first two segments of the abdomen dorsally.

Expanse 101 millim. ♀.

Hab. Rio Janeiro.

When the male is known, this species will require a new genus.

Othorene arpi. (Tab. III. fig. 7.)

Othorene arpi, Schaus, Proc. Zool. Soc. Lond. 1892, p. 289.

Male. Primaries deep yellow; the veins, inner and outer margins greyish, also a large triangular space extending along nearly the entire costal margin and defined by a darker line starting from the costal margin at one third from the base, and extending obliquely to the middle of the wing, from which point it returns to the costal margin near the apex; this greyish space becomes paler towards its extremity and includes a large yellow discal spot; a white spot at the base of the wings. Secondaries reddish. Body deep yellow; a grey and white spot on the first segment of the abdomen.

Expanse 70 millim.

Hab. Rio Janeiro, Brazil.

Othorene janeira. (Tab. III. fig. 9.)

Othorene janeira, Schaus, Proc. Zool. Soc. Lond. 1892, p. 289.

Male. Primaries deep yellow, tinged with purplish along the costal margin; fringe and veins dark grey; a dark grey line from the apex to the inner margin near the base, before reaching which it is joined by a basal grey line; at the base of the wings a large white spot. Secondaries deep yellow, red along the inner margin, and with a narrow dark transverse band. Body orange; reddish dorsally; a large white spot on the first segment.

Expanse 85 millim.

Hab. Rio Janeiro, Brazil.

Adelocephala invalida. (Tab. III. fig. 8.)

Adelocephala invalida, Schaus, Proc. Zool. Soc. Lond. 1892, p. 289.

Primaries above dark brown, tinged with purple; paler along the outer margin; a dark line, outwardly shaded with a slightly paler tint, from the apex to the middle of the inner margin; discal point white. Secondaries above dark red; fringe yellow. Underneath: primaries reddish; beyond the transverse line, which is purplish, the wing is yellow. Secondaries underneath yellow, speckled with reddish; a transverse reddish streak; reddish along the inner margin. Thorax and first segment of abdomen dorsally orange-red; abdomen otherwise dorsally purplish red, underneath yellowish white.

Expanse 42 millim.

Hab. Rio Janeiro.

Adelocephala columbia, sp. nov. (Tab. III. fig. 13.)

Primaries above brown, with a broad pinkish space at the base; a heavy pinkish shade from the apex to the middle of the inner margin; a small indistinct pinkish spot at the end of the cell. Secondaries reddish brown, with an indistinct dark transverse line from just within the apex on the costal margin to the middle of the inner margin. Underneath the wings are light reddish brown, with a broad pinkish shade on the outer margin of the primaries below the apex, and the outer margin of the secondaries is broadly pink. Thorax brown. Abdomen pinkish brown, somewhat tinged with red at the base.

Expanse 90 millim. ♀.

Hab. Columbia.

Citheronia vogleri. (Tab. III. fig. 2, ♂.)

Ceratocampa vogleri, Weyenb. Period. Zool. Arg. iii. p. 369 (1881).
Eacles leona, Druce, Proc. Zool. Soc. Lond. 1890, p. 500.

It affords me great pleasure to figure this fine and little-known species. I have compared my specimen with the type of *Eacles leona*, Druce, and find the species to be identical.

Fam. SATURNIIDÆ.

Automeris macareis. (Tab. III. fig. 3.)

Automeris macareis, Schaus, Proc. Zool. Soc. Lond. 1892, p. 290.

Male. Primaries brown, tinged with pinkish; darker beyond the outer transverse line, which extends from the middle of the inner margin to the apex; on this darker portion a marginal, wavy, lighter shade; a narrow basal transverse line; the discal spot finely outlined with dark brown. Secondaries pinkish brown; a little yellow between the ocellus and a transverse black line; the outer margin paler. The ocellus small, black, with a brownish centre containing a few white scales. Thorax brown. Abdomen reddish.

Expanse 70 millim.

The *female* is more of a pinkish grey; the space between the ocellus and transverse black line pink. Abdomen reddish brown, with broad black transverse bands.

Expanse 85 millim.

Hab. Petropolis, Brazil.

Automeris rubicunda. (Tab. III. fig. 1.)

Automeris rubicunda, Schaus, Proc. Zool. Soc. Lond. 1892, p. 290.

Male. Primaries above brown; the base fawn colour and limited by a very narrow, transverse, dark line; a lunular transverse line beyond the cell; the discal spot dark brown, oblong; a dark triangular spot on the costal margin near the apex. Secondaries above bright red; the ocellus small, black, with a brownish centre containing a few white scales; beyond this a black transverse line; a submarginal brownish band, and a marginal brownish shade on a paler ground. Underneath the primaries are yellowish, with a large black discal spot containing a white point; a submarginal dark lunular line. Secondaries underneath reddish brown, thickly speckled with black; a white discal point, and a transverse, lunular, brown line. Thorax brown, with posteriorly a number of white hairs. Abdomen reddish.

Expanse 54 millim.

Hab. Petropolis, Brazil.

This species is closely allied to *Automeris mendosa*, Boisd., which is well figured in the 'Biologia,' tab. 16. fig. 6, and the true habitat of which was not known till I captured a female on the Corcovado at Rio Janeiro.

Automeris rubrescens.

Hyperchiria rubrescens, Walk. Cat. Lep. Het. B. M. vi. p. 1281.

Larva. Length 3¼ inches when full-grown. Head prominent, bright green. Body green; laterally commencing at the fourth segment is a fold of skin below the stigmata; this is white, edged above with a fine black line; stigmata yellow; below the lateral fold and beginning between segments 4 and 5, and then between each successive segment, is a purplish patch dotted with white. Prolegs yellowish; abdominal legs outwardly purple dotted with white. Dorsally are four rows of long green spines having green branches; laterally are two short green spines on segments 2, 3, 4, 5, and 10, and on the other segments only a single spine which is still smaller. It spins a large pale brown silky cocoon, generally between leaves.

Pupa. Length 1⅜ inch, rather thick, dull black; wing-cases very slightly rough, but the thorax and head more so; on the latter, and also along the segments dorsally, are scattered a few very minute brown hairs. Began cocoons on Aug. 19th, and the first moths emerged on Sept. 24th.

Very common at Jalapa, Mexico.

Automeris saturata.

Hyperchiria saturata, Walk. Cat. Lep. Het. B. M. vi. p. 1282.
Hyperchiria schausii, H. Edw. Papilio, iv. p. 16.

Larva. Length $3\frac{1}{4}$-4 inches and rather stout in build. Head dull black. Body velvety black ; stigmata white. Dorsally are four rows of spines, except on the eleventh segment which has only three, the twelfth segment which has five, and the last segment which has none. Laterally, on segments 2, 3, 4, 5, 10, and 11 are two rows, and on segments 6, 7, 8, and 9 a single row of shorter spines. All the spines are yellow with yellow branches, except the following, which are entirely white—the four dorsal spines on segments 2 and 3, the inner two dorsal spines on segment 4, the three dorsal spines on segment 11, and the five on segment 12. The spines dorsally are of about equal length, except on the first two segments, where they are longer. Prolegs and abdominal legs shining black. Spins on the bark of trees a large leathery cocoon of a deep brown colour ; this at one end is especially thin and provided within with a perforated lid of the same texture, which is attached to the cocoon at one point only. The cocoons vary in length from $1\frac{1}{4}$-$2\frac{1}{2}$ inches and are very irregular in shape. The pupa is from 1 inch (♂) to $1\frac{3}{4}$ (♀) in length, and of a deep black. The thorax and head very rough, but the wing-cases very slightly so.

Extremely abundant at Banderilla, a short distance from Jalapa, Mexico.

Automeris zozine.

Automeris zozine, Druce, Biol. Centr.-Amer., Lep. Het. p. 179.

Larva. Length $1\frac{3}{4}$ inch. Very pale green ; dorsally four indistinct narrow yellowish bands, the outer ones faintly edged with maroon ; laterally, on segments 6 to 11, six large white spots, rather oblong in shape, and bordered above and below with maroon. Prolegs, abdominal legs, and anal lappet reddish. Dorsally four rows of green spines with green branches—on segment 12, however, only three. The dorsal spines on the first two segments are longer and tipped with black ; laterally a single entire row of spines and a smaller row below them on segments 2 to 6 and 11 to 13. Spins between dried leaves a thin and large cocoon of irregular shape.

Common at Jalapa and Coatepec, Mexico.

Molippa sabina.

Molippa sabina, Walk. Cat. Lep. Het. B. M. vi. p. 1345.

Larva. Length $2\frac{1}{2}$ inches. Head large, shining, deep red. Body light green, becoming yellowish before transforming ; dorsally are four rows of spines, which are longest on segments 2, 3, and 13 ; on segment 12 the two inner spines are replaced by a single subdorsal spine, and segment 13 has an extra subdorsal spine placed posteriorly. Stigmata white, edged with black ; laterally, below the stigmata, a row of short green spines and a smaller spine again below these on segments 2 to 6, 11, and 13.

Between the segments an irregular transverse band of black markings; subdorsally and centrally on each segment a black spot, and there are three little black lines between the inner and outer rows of dorsal spines. Between the lateral rows of spines is a broad black band extending the entire length, and having anteriorly and posteriorly on each segment a reddish spot; this extends somewhat underneath; otherwise underneath pale green. Prolegs, abdominal and anal legs reddish. Forms an oval and thin parchment-like cocoon on the bark of trees, usually under growing moss.

Both in the larval and imago state this species closely resembles the moth figured as *rivulosa* in Cramer, pl. 107 A, the larva of which is figured by Stoll, pl. 17. fig. 4, and eventually they may prove to be the same species. *Molippa sabina* is one of the commonest species in Tropical America, and in Mexico and Southern Brazil is double brooded.

I can see no reason for placing *Molippa*, *Ormiscodes*, *Hylesia*, *Dirphia*, and other allied genera from Tropical America under the Lasiocampidæ; these genera are too closely allied in all stages to *Automeris* and *Hyperchiria* to admit of "family" separation.

Ormiscodes opis. (Tab. IV. fig. 1.)

Ormiscodes opis, Schaus, Proc. Zool. Soc. Lond. 1892, p. 318.

Primaries above reddish brown; a basal straight, and an outer oblique, transverse grey band; a marginal wavy whitish shade; a long white streak at the end of the cell. Secondaries reddish brown; a median transverse greyish band and a submarginal dark brown shade. Underneath brown, the outer portion of the wings crossed by four bands of whitish scales. Head and thorax reddish brown. Abdomen black dorsally, whitish between the segments; anal segment red; underneath reddish brown.

Expanse 100 millim.

Hab. Petropolis, Brazil.

Lonomia carnica. (Tab. IV. fig. 2.)

Lonomia carnica, Schaus, Proc. Zool. Soc. Lond. 1892, p. 318.

Male. Above red, the wings crossed from the apex of the primaries to the middle of the inner margin on the secondaries by a broad black line, divided by a greyish shade; on the primaries two discal spots, the anterior one blackish, the posterior one white. Underneath pale brownish red, with broad marginal, paler shades; the transverse line very narrow and indistinct, inwardly shaded with white; on the primaries two white discal spots; on the secondaries a black discal spot circled with white; a large black spot at the apex.

Expanse 80 millim.

Hab. Petropolis, Brazil.

PLATE I.

Plate 1

1 HARRISINA JANEIRA
2 „   EMINENS.
3 PSEUDOMYA TIJUCA.
4 „   PELLUCIDA.
5 EUPYRA BACCHANS
6 „   PSITTACUS
7 „   CONSORS
8 „   AURATA
9 IOANTHRENE GAZA

10 GYMNELIA SERRA
11 COSMOSOMA HARPALYCE
12 DYCLADIA CATHERINA.
13   „   ROGENHOFERI
14   „   EPIMETHEUS
15 OARTHA DALSA
16 SYNTRICHURA DOERI.
17 ACLYTIA PETRA
18   „   HECALE.
19 CYANOPEPLA INACHIA.

20 HELIURA VENATA
21 EUPLESIA ELISSA
22 GALETHALEA PERUVIANA
23 THEAGES VESTALIS
24 METRIOPHYLA LENA
25 EUCEREON CLEMENTSI
26   „   LADAS
27 AMAXIA PYGA
28   „   HEBE

W Purkiss lith

1 DIAUS ORTUS
2 ABELES BYELIS
3 SCAPTUS CURIO
4 CISTHENE PETROVNA
5 TRICHOMELIA ORLENNA
6 EUDULE AURATA
7 " VENATA
8 ARDONEA METALLICA
9 GANGAMELA AYMARA
W. Purdom sk.

10 DARNA INOA
11 MENNIS SCEATA
12 " CYTHEREA
13 " UNA
14 SCEA SOLARIS
15 VIRBIA PARVA
16 BRYCEA PERUVIANA
17 YCES MAERA

18 NELO CAULLAMA
19 VIRBIA VARIANS
20 CYLLOPODA JANEIRA
21 " CHIRCHA
22 " DARNA
23 " QUICHA
24 LEUCOPSUMIS PALMEIRA
25 CYLLOPODA DUBIA
26 LEUCOPSUMIS BRAGANZA

PLATE III.

2

7

3

4

5

6

7

8

9

11

10

14

12

13

15

1 AUTOMERIS RUBICUNDA.	6 PHAEGOPTERA NOTATA	11 ECPANTHERIA PELLUCIDA, ♂
2 CITHERONIA VOGLERI	7 OTHORENE ARPI.	12 " " ♀
3 AUTOMERIS MACAREIS.	8 ADELOCEPHALA NIVALIDA.	13 ADELOCEPHALA COLUMBIA.
4 PHAEGOPTERA GRANIFERA	9 OTHORENE JANEIRA.	14 SYCHESIA JANEIRA.
5 SYSSISPHINX BASIREI	10 SYCHESIA HARTMANNI	15 PHAEGOPTERA URSINA.

W. Purkiss lith.　　　　　　　　　　　　　　　　　　　Hanhart imp.

1.